TEST FLIGHTS

TEST FLIGHTS

poems by

KERRY PAUL MAY

West End Press

Grateful acknowledgment is made to the following publications in which some of these poems originally appeared:

Anthology of Magazine Verse & Yearbook of American Poetry, Eugene Writer's Anthology, Fireweed, Jam To-Day, Kingfisher, New England Review/Breadloaf Quarterly, Northwest Review, Pacifica Awards Magazine, Portland Review, Rhino, Three Rivers Poetry Journal, Willowsprings.

First edition, January 1995
ISBN 0-931122-79-1

Front cover photograph provided by the author
Back cover photograph by Lucena Monical
Cover art concept by Doug Brashear
Cover produced by Michael Reed
Book design by Michael Reed
Typography by Prototype, Albuquerque, NM

Distributed by The Talman Company, Inc.
131 Spring Street, Suite 201 E-N
New York, NY 10012
(212) 431-7175
FAX (212) 431-7215

West End Press • P.O. Box 27334 • Albuquerque, NM 87125

Contents

V.

VI.

VII.

IN MEMORY OF MY FATHER

I.

The Shave

From his chair, in the corner
Of the aseptic, white Dead Room,
He watches his father sleeping,
Oxygen steaming from beneath
His plastic nose mask, his body
Slack from the solvents he had
Once dipped the large turbine
Engine parts into as he floated
Above the fumes, his thick arms
Now withered to bone from cobalt
And platinum, the slow drowning
Rising from inside his chest.
An hour before, in awakening,
His father asked, would he shave
Him, run his electric over his
Cheeks until the smoothness he knew
Each morning before work returned
And maybe to leave this world
Clean-shaven might be a good thing
And worth the risk, to go out
As he arrived, clean, smooth and small.
So he took his father's face into
His hands, a face he had only
Recently learned to touch as his
Own, the stunned love discovered
In remission and ran the electric
Over his skin, following with finger-
Tips, searching the smooth surfaces
For the errant bristles, perfecting
Awkward into ease, until his father
Told him, Good, and he sits once
More, a book propped in his hands
That now smell like his father's
Face and recalls the snapshot sent
From Alaska, his father's first beard
That flowed rich and black against
His age, and the letter written,
How the Northern Lights outside
His Quonset hut were indeed
The most beautiful things but one

Could watch only briefly in such
Cold as was found on Point Barrow
But the coffee was always hot
And one shouldn't have to ask
For much more from life than this.
His father sleeps as he reads.
Then, with first one hand, then
The other, he brings them up to
His own cheeks. He closes his eyes
And believes it's his father's face
He's touching, haloed in the fur lining
Of his parka hood, the light show,
Beyond the radar huts focused on
Russian skies, enormous, almost holy,
Touching his father's face, still touching.

Poachers, 1963

Mother is dressed in red.
A venison roast bubbles
In the oven. The grown-ups
Hold vigil in the kitchen.
The kitchen fills with smoke.
Talk comes from whiskey—
Autumn's elusive black herds,
The early, heavy snow when
Chuck and Tom nearly dis-
Appeared, that crazy goddamn
Rosie emptying his Luger,
Out of frustration, into
A porcupine until it sparkled.
The TV rolls, Times Square lit
In ashy, wind-bent reception
And we're up late, underfoot.
How to explain the four-point
That appeared two nights ago,
Skinned and gutted in Father's
Garage, the twisted grillwork,
Shattered headlamp, the men
Working all night while strays
Whimpered outside the door,
The state trooper packing
Flank steaks into the trunk
Of his cruiser this morning?
The steady din of New Year's
Rises to the ceiling. When
The roast is sliced we're each
Given a slab and shooed outdoors.
The slices are thick and tender.
The glaze, burnt and sweet.
On a dare, who can hold
A clove longest beneath
Their tongue. Mother is dressed
In red. She's a knockout.
The lipstick she wears
Is Jackie's favorite shade—
Support for the nation's widow.
The head White House chef

5

Has resigned, the menus changed.
The new decor begins in a week.
Grease clings to my fingers
Like a lie. It won't come clean.

Roses, 1964

1.

She's in the kitchen, where the men
Of that time thought all women
Should be, drying the supper
Dishes, alone in the house where
Her husband had grown into
A man, raising chickens, repairing
Fences, weeding the forever garden
While his brothers, one younger,
One older, went about their
Lives. This is the kitchen where
Cabbage is cooked, the aroma
Permeating the curtains, wedged
Into the oval doorway seams,
Where the politics of the New
Deal were hushed before begun
And lunch pails were lined up
At the sink by their departure
Times. The sons and their father
Have gone to the hospital to
Be with the woman who no longer
Knows them, the cancer evolved
Into her brain stem, to spend their
Hours watching her embroidering
The pillowcases of air, darning
The hundreds of socks passed
Down from son to son to son.

2.

December is the wrong time to die.
Too many details, the holidays
Forthcoming. In the house,
Paperchains from childhood,
Fresh popcorn and cranberries.
No one expects to go like this,
The hands acting on their own,
The faces coming and going,
The names erased by a shadow,
The bed sheets changed hourly.
The woman in the kitchen
Is making a list, not because
She's forgetful, but to organize,
To keep creativity alive, to
Block out what's approaching.
And there's music playing
On the living room phonograph,
Maybe Bing Crosby or young
Andy Williams, her favorite.
The dishes are done. She sits
At the table where the brothers
Sat an hour before eating
The meal she had prepared.
When the music ends the house
Is quiet, as it should be. Today
More snow has fallen, the Wasatch
Range humbled in white gowns.
Traffic hushes by on the street.

3.

Any other time it would be
Perfect. She sits, makes her list
Of ideas, meals, gifts, games,
And the room suddenly fills
With the rich scent of roses
And somehow she knows it's over,
Her husband's mother is gone.
She makes note of the time.
She doesn't know how she knows.
Roses don't happen every day.
The kitchen was her room, holidays
Planned, birthdays organized,
Where the middle son had her forge
His father's signature on his
Government induction papers
For his stretch in the Pacific—
The scent enough to swoon by.
Then, just as quickly, it's gone.
What's left to do? Dishes done,
Leftovers wrapped and stored—
She's in the kitchen, where the men
Of that time thought all women
Should be. For this time, only this
One time, she's happy it is so—
Two women, in roses, filling the room.

                    —for my mother

A War

One night, hearing noises
In the kitchen, going down,
I saw him, shirtless, before
The open refrigerator, light
Glowing on his boyish face.
He was lifting covers
From the plates and bowls,
Jabbing his thick fingers
Into applesauce, butter,
Gravy, rice, then carefully
Replacing the plastic wrap.
I saw it all. My brother-
In-law knew some things—
Soldiering, hand-to-hand,
And instinct. When he sensed
Me, he turned, his left
Forearm up and set to fly,
Then sat me down quick,
And paced the floor. "Do
You know where I'm going?"
He asked me. I did not.
Somewhere else. Away. A war.
I'd swear to this—the manly
Way he drank my father's
Beer, how he'd slowly shake
His head at his lousy luck,
But put a finger to his lips.
And each night that week
Before he shipped out I knew
It was him in the kitchen,
Standing in the soft light,
Cool air fanning his bare
Chest, tasting pork chop, milk,
Macaroni, on his fingertips,
Praying, raiding, savoring,
Feasting on his own goodbyes.

_____ II. _____

Willamette Pass

Far back,
Beyond a million slender pines,
The moon hangs frozen
As an October apple.
The slumbering air
Weaves the sweet traces
Of screw-cap wine
Through our fuselage of old bones.
High above Ashland
Our driver eases his large shadow
Outside into moonlight
For mailbags, runaways and cigarettes,
Then circles us, slowly,
Tapping the tire chains.

The Good Ones

In her old souvenir photo book,
"Touring the Oregon Highway,"
She had circled, in red, a spot
Off the motorway, deep in the trees,
Because she had picnicked there once
With her one true love, a tall
Pennsylvania man, one afternoon in
The summer of nineteen twenty-seven.
Her bonnet was bunched to her stickpin,
Her elbow gloves were silky white,
And her skirts ruffled in the breeze.
It was when goggles were the fashion
And rumble seats opened and shut
Like small coffins. And after a lunch
Of chicken salad, rolls, lemonade,
And homemade gin, he took her,
Right there, on the gingham cloth,
A total of three times. She wanted
Him to. But, there was never such
Talk as marriage. Sport was in
The young woman's blood. What she
Conceded to, oh, much later in
Her life, was a sentiment, how
The good ones always got away.
She clipped his poems from the news
Until her hatbox was full.
And now the original highway is closed,
Sectioned off, unsafe for today's speed.
It looks ancient, something Roman
Or Greek. And on my way
To a hometown of truth and pain
I pass by the same spot she
Had circled and I think of her
Brief romance, deep in the trees,
And of her, the way she must have
Turned her head so the afternoon light
Caught the finest features of her hair,
The genuine bliss of her encouraging grin.

Night Cutting

Whatever it is, however it comes,
it takes time—
—Stanley Plumly

At that moment, stepping out
Of your car into the oranging
August air, nothing else mattered—
Not the stars tense in blackness,
Not the dust tearing your eyes,
Not the years stinging your memory
Like the last taste of flesh on your tongue. . . .
From a distant road you saw
Headlights, three huge combines
Creeping across the final hillside
Of wheat, three trucks clanking
Slowly alongside. The drivers,
Half in and half out of their cabs,
Shifted and steered as their beds
Were loaded with grain.
What was it? A new loneliness,
This scene forgotten by all
But these workers, their pace
Born four generations before them?
Or one more style of romance, timid,
Like the air before a hailstorm?
The workers killed their engines
And stood down. In a circle,
Shaking hands, the harvest ended.
Nothing would matter. Whatever
It was you knew it would take time.
For when they turned away,
Toward home, they remained there,
Ascendant (you saw them) and alone.

Two Months Sober, a Farmer Walks into October

Beside the new blond corral
He listens to the soft click of his cattle
Huddling together in the moonlight.
Beneath his feet he feels
The delicious crunch of gravel
As he walks toward his father's father's house.
Now his own shadow,
Pressed into the earth from a high floodlight,
Is enough to accompany him home.
He turns back, listens. Barn swallows
Swirl the rich night air. He touches
His clean, smooth face with both hands,
Then turns again, continues walking,
As all things begin shaping themselves.

Autumn in Eastern Oregon

The wind renews
Its brute warnings
In the tall, faded
Plateau grasses.
Sunlight is lynched
In afternoon grays.
Thunderheads bale
The western range.
The last cricket
Of the season avenges
Its short, brown life
With whiskery sentences
In wing-song.
In the long shadows
Of great grain silos
A Paiute ghost walks,
His shoulders heavy,
Along the wheat-
Scattered road. His
Presence stirs dimension,
That lost grace.
If I called out
He would turn, slowly,
And feel dark November
Flicker through his body,
His stony hair.

—for Ralph

Beyond

A child's waking cry . . . and I rise
From dead sleep to see the high, round hills
Coated with heavy snow and moonlight.

Another cry. I dress and move, quietly,
Through the cool parlor, all others
Asleep in the great house, until, there,

Just outside the kitchen window, atop
The fat, silver heating oil tank,
I spot the sound makers, huddled
Side by side, a male and his mate.

They've burrowed their plump bodies
Into a drifted mound of snow for warmth.
They've settled in against the plateau wind

That carries their winter cries down
Through nearby canyons that I explored
On my summer walks, and along
The freshly plowed highway, and farther,

Beyond this clear, chilled December night,
Beyond the moonlight and white cover,
Beyond my desire to hold them, tenderly,
Two peacocks, watching me watching them.

—for Jeanie

42 Below

Twenty steps from the yellow light
He wanted to lie down, to sleep.
He entered the farmhouse, so polite,
Pardon me, he said, and lay before
The oil stove. I was alone, assembling
Christmas toys, an uncle's duty.
The stranger entered, convinced
Of his death, wild-eyed, frightened.
I could smell the sweet angel
Of alcohol floating above him.
Quiet, unimposing, he lay still.
I thought of driving into a white-out
Until the road fell away, of walking
Toward a light on a hill, my layers
Of wool abandoning themselves to wind,
And of sleep warming my thighs.
But took up wrench, screwdriver
And diagrams and resumed to build,
Listening to the stranger's now steady
Breathing slowly filling the house—
Closed my eyes. Together we rocked.

                                    —for Norm

History

Alone in the great house
The small voices of nieces
Still fill the cold parlor
Corners, the vacant spaces
Now beneath the lighted tree.
Today an angry man lies
In a perfect rectangle
Sliced in the frozen ground.
The man died from piling
Stones, one by one, loading
A wagon, clearing his land.
A man can die in agony
From the fat hand of God
Or be struck by lightning,
Like my uncle, after his day
In the fields, his swaying
Hayrack torched all down
To its wheels, his horses
Kneeled down, the blue smoke
Rising off their broad backs—
My uncle snatched up by
The seat of his pants then
Laid to his quick calling,
Twenty-seven paces away,
The aroma of fresh biscuits
And stew clouding his house,
His wife on the screened porch,
A ladle pressed to her lips. . . .
Midday, thirty-two below,
Ice flowers form on the windows
Until the centerpanes bloom.
In the silent house a clock
Ticks like a farmer's heart.
The Christmas whiskey is gone.
The oil stove kicks over
Gasping for its jellied heat.
An angry man is put to rest.
Yet, I claim no part in his
Affairs. An outsider, a stranger
From the city—I've grown away

From here. But soon, after
The family returns, I'll take
My place in the warm kitchen
And listen to the women talk.

Farmer

It's a matter of wind.
That farmhouse leans deeper
Into the plateau each year
I return. But not this year.
The plateau will have to weather
Its assault without me,
The farmhouse, its lacy bruise.
I won't come up from the river
In October to measure the shift
Of its angle in the sunlight.
I'm through with giving hope
To the topsoil that seeps
From beneath its foundation.
Not even the lovers' graffiti
Carved into its boarded windows
Can lure me up from the water.
The wind can have it, can
Take the paint chips and bones
Down into the canyons with its runoff.
The weather vane can twist
Its hard sentence forever alone.
And heat lightning that plucks
The Holsteins from the hillside trails
Can turn the dirt pathways
Into glass, burn the lupine
Like a beacon to its god. See,
It's a matter of wind.

—for John

The Pumphouse

Better to watch from the dry porch,
Rain washing down each side of the house,
Shags of light rippling through low clouds.
Thunder steals all toll paintings
From their perches.
Peacocks float to their eaves.
On the horizon the pumphouse accepts
The force like the first warnings
Of a blind man rounding a corner
Clinging to the volume of his tapping.
It catches the full tide.
Better to imagine rain pressed
Into its wooden walls than be stung
By its swarm as the storm leaps from hill
To battered hill.
The pumphouse leans into the soft earth.
Each wave runs listlessly down
The ribs of its rooted body.
Better you are here, on the dry porch,
Watching, changing,
Every day the rest of your working life.

_____ III. ____

Test Flight

A neighbor is up early.
In housecoat and slippers
She waters her walkway
Of shrubbery pausing at
Each thick-rooted stem.
She's edged and trimmed
Creating a perfect geometry
Bordered around her home.
Night has sweated out of
Her landscaped elms into a
Dewy plastic across her
Smooth butch-cut lawn.
Today she'll fix her hair,
Buy a peach-colored blouse,
Thaw a pork roast—
Her movements are as precise
As her years, that fall,
Like her breasts, or the fine
Skin beneath her eyes.
What has it come to?
A rumor as continental as rain?
It's turned so damn silly.
She twists the spigot
And coils the hose,
Then looks up at the blue
Sliced by vapor threads
Heading east, a test flight
Longing for Nebraska. Her
Gaze moves sadly from house
To house in the cul-de-sac.
She focuses on her porch steps
Where the dust of her pale
Tired body would glow,
Her whole darkened form
Flaming, then cooling, then
Cold. And all around her
Nothing could grow. Nothing.
Nothing at all could grow.

Remember

After midnight great semis
Swing down 13th Avenue
Dragging one, two, three
Trailers behind their clamor,
The only hours city police
Grant such passage through.
Glimmer, but no horn blast,
The cowardly freightlines exit
For Idaho, Montana, Utah—
Chicken pies, toilet tissue, hibachis,
Whatever it takes to get there.
A slight blackened dust,
Like ash, festoons the local
Proprietors' winter walk-ups,
A hustling wind sprint before
Sunrise shuts them down cold.
On the interstates they bully
The rest stops, negotiate E.T.A.s—
A hundred towns ahead smaller
Than the hundreds left behind.
A chauffeur of fresh hot waste
Plots his course, where
To dump his crude load,
Which asphalt stretch to
Anchor the sludge—places
Where he'd never bivouac,
Not on his life, and how, who-
Ever it is, thumb out, walking
The gravelly fringe, would
Never know what hit him,
Remember where, remember when.

Sirens

Put yourself in her shoes,
An unusually warm Saturday
Evening in February, stepping
Out of Jones' Market with her
Small bag of groceries, seeing
No traffic all along 13th Avenue
And it being just moments beyond
Twilight. The cloud cover over
The city was illuminated with
Street lights, movie theatre
Marquees and apartment towers,
Creating a kind of glow one
Can associate with flames. She
Stopped dead in her tracks when
The sirens began, three, four,
She couldn't tell, coming from
All directions, a low whine
At first then louder as if
Converging but to no definite
Place, all around her. And once
More the grade school drills
Came back to her, her classmates
And her huddled under their
Little desks, her hands over her
Ears, her eyes closed for that short
Emergency until the bells in
The hallways ceased their ringing
And her teacher emerged above her
Desk and clapped her hands so
They would all rise and take
Their seats and proceed with their
Science or history lesson. Like
Nothing happened. But outside Jones'
She froze, only for seconds,
Which was long enough to remind
Her that she had no desk to
Crawl under and that it wouldn't
Matter much, really, and those
Who would make it through this
Would find the shape of a woman

Standing out on a sidewalk holding
Her small bag of oranges, coffee
And cheese with something like
A sneer on her face and looking
Up at the sky and maybe
Pointing at what was there.

Tar Smoke

Today I watched some workers
Tarring my neighbor's roof.
They were bare chested; long
Hair wrapped with bandanas,
Smoke had turned their arms
And faces black, like yours must
Have been on night patrol.
They were your age, younger,
Drinking on their breaks,
Smoking in my neighbor's shade.

I'd seen the photos and films.
My teachers commended your fall.
You were a first-rate punk,
A quick-buck artist knuckling
My head, a huckster— So
Little left of you to send home.

The young men worked
All afternoon, breathing tar,
Their bare chests shining,
Then revving husky cars after
Knocking off, like you, hungry
For fast machines and dates
Willing to overlook the city lights.

They brought you back, Michael—
Your mother in a housecoat
Weeping on her front steps,
The two escorts watching sadly.
Your young wife and two boys
Beginning, already, to take wrong
Turns—but your checks arrived
Each month, your ID tags lost,
Swinging from a tree limb,
Somewhere, over there.

I thought of you, whole, like
The smart-ass that you were.
Not even you could tell this
Was all wrong. And for that
Moment, caught up in myself,

Myself and you, you not knowing
You'd fail to return, I began
Believing that somehow, when
This summer evening cooled,
You'd walk out of that jungle
To find your name on the Wall.

                —for Pfc Michael Clayton,
                                d. 1968

IV.

The Bracelet

Evening beneath the high green cover
Of the aspens at the Motel Osuna
Comes on earlier than expected
And no one is more surprised
Than my sister diving for pieces
Of Franco's silver in the leaf-strewn
Pool that bears the great face
Of the sun that is Spain, 1969,
When Vietnam thunders night after
Night down Torrejon's flight line
And the silver bracelet she wears,
Bearing a name she'll never know,
Catches the glow of the restaurant
Each time she rises from the water
And ignites the white tree trunks
Creating a fire for the faceless
Pilot she refuses to lose hope for.

—for Col. Norman Eaton,
MIA 1/13/69

35

Sevilla

He walks alone. He is an old man.
In black beret his heavy breath
Blooms across the empty plaza.

He stops and cocks his head.
Quietly he taps his olive walking
Stick against the clean, white

Cobblestones. He counts the echoes.
He taps a little louder. Again, he
Listens. The names rush over him.

Where is his captain? It's 6 a.m.
He checks the alleys for shadows.
Nothing. He is an old man. It was

A long time ago. So, he shoulders
His walking stick and slowly scans
The rooftops. Whatever moves is dead.

—for Eduardo

The Descent

What can you dream to make Time real again?
—Robert Penn Warren

Looking down from Paracuellas,
Small condemned village high above
Field after swollen field
Of stone, I could see nothing
But whiteness, the valley bed
Covered with motionless morning
Fog. This was heaven, up here,
This place of brackish plaster
Walls, rutted streets—where
Children raced the passing cars
Like thin-ribbed Gypsy greyhounds,
Where women with deep black
Scars for eyes called out
From inside their beaded stoops,
Where thickly muscled men
Thumbed their flat noses
At all passersby while peeling
Yams into tin buckets
That could not give life back to
The village's only crumbling well.
And below, the road invisible.
Heaven. Shepherds took their
Daily count with brassy whistles
Then listening. A radio station
Stood above the cloud cover,
Its red beacon burning. I
Had hitchhiked to this presence
When the driver, an American sergeant,
Stopped his sleek orange Fiat
Atop Paracuellas and we both
Stood among the thieves
And prostitutes to witness
This calm, this brutal penance.
Heaven, yes. Time's dream was real.
And moments later we pitched
The fast-closing villagers
A handful each of coins,
Our feeble defense, because we

Could, because it was their country,
Theirs, not ours. And we climbed
Back into our seats, shaken,
A shower of stones and sticks,
To descend, the sergeant's
Thin fist jammed white
Against the Fiat's tiny horn.

The Tourists

It was a fine day. Just right
For short sleeves and sandals.
The man sat sipping iced limón
Watching the finest hookers
From Germany, Switzerland and,
Thinking he heard the proper
Accent, from France, as they made
Their way up from the beaches,
Through the plaza. Every summer
They come to Barcelona to rest,
To take leave of the northern
Winters, perhaps to pick up a fare
Or two, but mostly to rest, to
Enjoy labor's own fruit. The man
Would like to offer one of them
An evening out. Perhaps a night
With real experience would do him
Some good. He could rent a car
And drive up to a surrounding
Hill, park, watch the city lights
Below and let her do her thing
To him, whatever it was. Perhaps.
The thought excites him. He
Begins to examine the women walking
Slowly by with a bit more scrutiny.
It's always been a matter of being
Seen with someone nice looking.
Besides, she'd be making a buck.
And so it goes—this one for her
Narrow hips, that one, strawberry
Hair—until racket from a corner
Tavern turns everyone's head
To see a small man, his face
Bloodied, one long sleeve of his
Hawaiian print sport shirt torn
Clean off, dangling from his wrist,
Pick himself up off the cobble
Street and make his way toward
A fountain and dip his sleeve into
The water and bring it up to his

Swollen nose. Then the small man
Puts his whole head into the water,
Raises up, slicks back his hair.
He wrings his sleeve out, tucks
It into his pocket. He turns, sees
Everyone looking at him. "What?"
He shouts and the onlookers
Turn back to their own business.
The man sipping his cool drink
Resumes his task of selecting
Just the right woman for himself.
It's then he sees the small man
With one sleeve stop and speak
To a woman with high breasts
And large hands carrying a blue
Fishnet shoulder bag. The small
Man reveals his money clip, thick
With bills. He holds up four
Fingers. The woman reaches down
And cups the weight of his crotch
With her free hand. She holds
Up five fingers. He agrees, hooks
Her arm in his (the arm with
The remaining good sleeve), hails
A taxi, climbs in beside her,
And is gone, leaving behind him
The man with his empty glass,
Who only then breathes in
The mixture of rich aromas
Coming from the cafés that line
The street and sees, with sunset
But an hour away, how the waiters
Have begun to set up the tables
And chairs which will soon halt
All traffic and the tourists who
Spend the warm afternoon napping
In their rooms will rise, dress
For dinner, come down, and eat.

The Arrival

In July's floozy shade,
Beneath the pine green netting
Of a small roadside bodega,
Our long month of touring ended.
In northern Spain once more,
Adjusting to the high, raw light
And such indifferent clockwork,
We were happy for the chance
To lean back and let a red
Basque wind swirl the fine dust
Around us, darkening our sweaty
Shirts. My father raised his tall
Henniger beer and pressed its
Cold kiss against his forehead
Then drank deeply before closing
His eyes, locking his fingers across
His heart and let sleep lure him in.
Not before and not since
Have I loved my father more
Than at this moment, watching him,
His adventurous middle age—
Not when his last breath flitted
Warmly in my ear, not when his
Grip tightened on my arm, then
Went soft, not when the young
Brown cricket leaped into his
Grave. And, but for our nervous
Proprietor, who measured olives
And peanuts into finger plates
(We were his first Americans),
The old village wavered in swift
Heat and each pale, dull home,
Built into the bare, shallow hills
That surrounded this sleeping
Man, sunk back and fused again
With the hard clay, with the wind,
With the rumor of rain the villagers
Would speak of to come now that
Strangers had arrived without warning.

Last Meeting, Plaza Mayor

Not lonely, reader. No.
But, coaxed by summer,
I sat in the general's
Lengthening shadow that
Drifted slowly across
The leafy, iron tables
Into my tumbler of
Iced anisette, and, for my
Long hair and blue jeans,
Came under the watchful eyes
Of the general's black-
Booted Civil Guard, who
Clicked their holster snaps
Beneath their shoulder capes
And circled me with great
Care, when from deep inside
"Las Cuevas," a cluster of
Schoolboys emerged into
The plaza, faces flushed,
Victorious, their futbol
Sweaters knotted sloppily
Around their necks, spitting.
They gave me the finger,
"¡Hijo de puta!" their
Triple-rhythmic flamenco
Claps echoing off the rust-
Stained masonry, off the dull,
Weathered, shopkeeper's gates,
Until landing sternly
Across my smooth, turned cheek
As they marched before me
Then disappeared into
The street. And I waited,
Knowing that my friend and I
Would be happy in our shame-
Less, American denim,
Walking in Madrid's quiet air,
The soft, yellow lighting
Of its million alleyways,
Low-rent kitchens a kind

Of canvas for our dreams
Of careers assumed for us
Back in The World— I'd tell
My friend how the stiff-
Necked waiters cooed my
Simple wealth as they moved
Between the tables, their
Trays held outstretched, poised
On their scrubbed fingertips,
Their short, white jackets
Dancing in the long bronze
Of the general's shadow like
Candlestubs for El Cordobés.

          —for Don, 1974

_____ V. ____

Autumn

The woman sits looking out
The café window and is having
Herself a smoke and a coffee.
She has dished up enchiladas
And diet sodas all afternoon
And needs some private time,
A moment to sit and stare out
At all the curled-up leaves
Twirling across the semi-busy
Four-lane. Lipstick appears,
Suddenly, on the filter tip
Of her slim cigarette, on
The rim of her paper cup.
She weighs some other autumn—
More than the fact the air
Was crisp, the sky was blue,
The earth beginning to cool.
There is romance in her face
When I enter the empty café
And she calls, Hello,
Gives me coffee, then sits again,
To watch the bright leaves
Cartwheeling in the street,
Awhile longer,
Before her angel comes.

The Viewing

Far below, on the river
Trolling near its banks,
Were two sails, one blue,
One white. It was April
And overcast in the city,
The aspens beginning to
Green, and the other street-
Walkers, who'd shed last
Night's rain on Grant, now,
Too, rose in strange beds
As I stood on the balcony
Of the doctor's son's house
While the coffee brewed,
The Sunday breakfast traffic
Yet to be significant,
The horseback patrolmen
Still currying their flanks.
Across the river the new,
Pink crematorium rose in
Morning light. I gripped
The cold iron railing and
Witnessed two perfect plumes
Of smoke rising from her twin
Chimneys, a sparkled haze
Of flesh, bones and hair,
First rising up then drifting
Down, settling among the trees
By the river, among the homes
On this street of dreams, of
Circular driveways, frosty
Milk bottles perched at their
Gates and hedges clipped into
Diamond shapes. I rocked
To keep my presence firm—
Sundays, they burn on Sundays—
Then stepped back inside
The doctor's son's house
And latched out the cold
And poured myself the first
Of many cups, and sat at

His kitchen table, and smoked
His cigarettes, and determined
That the fifty-dollar bill
This punk had stuffed into
The lounge singer's brandy
Snifter, last night at dinner,
Was only money, then left
Before the doctor's son awoke.

In an hour I felt better.

Photo

The soldier on the front page
Has his arm around a small boy
Who's eating a mash of grain
Vitamins and honey.
Note how tightly the boy holds
On to the soldier's sleeve
As if, should he let go,
This man in the metal hat
And coat that looks like autumn leaves
Would depart with his whispered name
And powdered milk—
Perhaps it's a Tuesday,
An hour before work,
And the photo you're looking at
Stays with you
The rest of your day, your week.
Everywhere you turn
The soldier and the boy
Are there, before you.
You can't shake
What is passing between these two
In the photographer's lucky moment.
And it follows you.
And it breaks your fucking heart,
The image, the very idea—
The small boy holding his bowl,
The soldier holding him up
To steady his world as he eats.

This Couple

It starts with something simple—
Cashing a check, spending the night,
The easy division of laundry chores.
Yet, they forge ahead—he, slouched
To her abstract aggression, she,
Bemused by his anger, control.
Once, it was November, overcast,
A late afternoon, people pushing
Against the low sky—I believe
It must have been a Friday by
The tempo of life—they stepped
Off the Glenwood bus in loud dis-
Cussion, she giving him the "what-for,"
And he, witnessed by his posture, in
Complete denial, cutting her remarks
Firmly as spoken until she slapped
Him, pulled her hand back, caught
His full, unshaven cheek, palm
Cupped so as to be heard above
The six-lane Franklin traffic,
Snapping his head nearly around,
Dislodging his hearing aid. And for
A moment everything stopped—the late-
Staying flickers on their black wires,
The dwarf pine cones rolling toward
Winter, the echoes of after school,
Hardwood gymnasium floors. . . . Then
She turned quickly toward swing shift
Trailing her apron, and he, at first
Stunned, standing alone, as other
Passengers moved wide around his
Island, his cheek no doubt burning,
Left ear ringing, until pocketing
His bony fists and following behind,
At a distance, but keeping pace.

_____ VI. _____

Navajo Winter

It's late November. Something
Stirs in the tall, graying weeds
In the alley behind the leaning
White shed. Is someone there?
Could it be the same wind
That once lifted the black hat
From my great-grandfather's head
And sent it straight up into
The clouds? Or the white breath
Of Joseph's people when surrender
Assured many autumns yet to be?

My grandfather, whistling inwardly,
Sits alone in the garage doorway
Looking out at November tumbling
Over the miles of tract housing.
He cracks the walnuts he gathered
From the large tree in the yard
Then measures the nut meats
Into one-pound paper sacks
For the widows up the street
Who invite him to tea.

Each November I can believe
How I am one-quarter
Of my grandfather's blood.
And yet wonder, could it be
An arm or a leg, or my receding
Hairline that shelters this proof.
Or none of these things but
Something that lies just beneath
My skin. The wind slips down
From Canada and is cold.
The ground hardens into sleep.
And the pulse in the long roots
Of our brothers, the trees, has slowed.

Were I dressed in heavy blankets
Woven by the mother of us all
I would face the wind bravely.
But do not. But listen to what

Moves in the weeds, in the alley,
Slowly settling in—slowly, like my
Grandfather, moving about beneath
The large tree before sunrise,
Gathering the tiny planets lying
In the grass, then warming each,
Briefly, in his large, brown hands.

—for The Great Indian,
my grandfather, John P. Cordero

A Late Portrait of My Father

At the kitchen counter
He carves a peach into
Small pieces then brings them,
One by one, to his mouth
And chews slowly, then waits
To see if it stays down.
If not, he leans over
The sink then wipes his lips
And tries another piece.
He's telling his body
That he's still in control,
That nothing can take this
Simple function away
From him, the cool sweetness
Of fruit from his shrinking
Tongue. Tomorrow he will
Attempt a pear, apple,
Or plums, and, like now, lose
Most of it, but still carve
And eat until he tires
Of standing. Embarrassed, he turns
His head to cough. He asks
Me the same questions as
This morning, nodding at
My replies. Good peaches,
He says when he turns in
Leaving all lights burning.

Winter

The books twist back on their spines.
Opened, the dust from the shelves
Of the shop where they were bought
Reaches my nostrils—not mold,
But a money scent, a suit and tie,
Jimmy's uniform back from the Nam,
A closet of funeral-going garments.
Now a thick piece of pine turns
In the woodstove, showing its red ribs.
My cat, Willow, rests her gray chin
On my leg as I read, drink coffee
And smoke beneath the only lamp
Still burning in the shifting house.
She reaches out her paw, lightly,
To stretch, to keep me awake, claws
Gently piercing through my sleeve.
The books twist and glower. Winter
Stacks them beside my favorite chair.
The house shifts. Wind catches the screens
Rattling the eye hooks. Fire snaps
And dies down. And somewhere a man
Is dancing on the eastward interstate,
On black ice, beside his jackknifed
Semi and trailer. In steel-toed boots
He dances in his triangle of flares
Above a river slowly freezing over,
A sound much like the sex of his
Ancestors who brought him here, to
This place, this time, this life.

                              —for Sgt. James B. Carlson,
                                        d. 8/68

The Gift

What had you hoped to gain, son?
A trophy? The gift of fresh meat?
You knew the elk would gather
Just below, grazing on the last
Green shoots of grass before they
Descend further to the valleys,
Hard prairies and lake beds. There
Was nothing to stop you from
Sighting in on the largest bull,
A six-point, his antlers clean
And smooth, his coat already
Thickened, heavy with winter fat.
From his center of seven cows
He had arced his large headdress
And surveyed the dim afternoon
Light evading the sparse treeline
For a scent of anything that
Moved. There was nothing to keep
You from squeezing off three good
Rounds into his heart or throat,
Just like I taught you on all
Those weekend trips together,
Such blasts you knew for sure would
Drop him quickly and without pain.
There was nothing, nothing, that is,
But him alone when he turned your
Way and held his stare, not chewing,
His ears cocked, his eyes unflinching,
No twitch, no steam breath drifting
From his fine black snout. Maybe
It was glare from your gun barrel,
The fire of your fluorescent vest,
Your round outline frozen against
The flat treeless skyline he saw,
Or your own pulsing breath. But
He dropped his head once again,
Unconcerned. And it was there, in
Your sights, that you saw something
Only a few will have chance to see—
The dark, quiet herd making their

Slow way down from the mountain,
Into the approaching winter, alive.

—b. 1925, d. 1985

_____ VII. ____

Fate

Tonight I take down the poet's books,
Stack them neatly, and begin from his
Beginning, rewording the reviews I'd
Written, the kindness I'd passed on.
There were negatives, but I let them go.
I, too, know the failure of long nights,
The triumph of a few good hours,
Like putting on slippers and stepping
Out into January then returning inside
To the warmth with an armful
Of perfect split oak. It's April now.
The cherry blossoms in the dentist's
Parking lot drift like snow across
The Reserved slots. Firewood for my
Schrader stove is diminished to new
Business for the cutters from Creswell,
Who park their pickup loads at Safeway—
There, that's it. Simple. How some lives
Cross paths indeterminately, what
The poet would have called fate—
A dentist, a woodcutter, the blossoms
Doing their thing, the one or two good
Nights when, his arms loaded with quarter-cuts,
His lover says, without looking up,
"Did you remember the carport light?"
Then says, "Here, now. Let me handle that."

—In memory, Raymond Carver

63

Cambodia

In the dentist's parking lot,
Just after dawn,
The old woman rotates her arms,
First forward then back.
She bends at the waist
As far as she can. She holds,
Breathes, then begins again.
Her tunic is faded jade, floral,
Her wrists slender as reeds.
I believe in her hard witness
As she exercises her right
To a defensive religion,
Can see into her ocean,
The darkness out beyond
Her teetering boat,
Heavy with families,
Black water quickly spilling in—
Each morning since midsummer
She's come here to pray
This life in America.
She strikes her pose,
Rubs her palms together, rapidly,
Then presses them to her temples.
She offers her face
To the October sunlight,
Slowly bends her knees. Holds.
Breathes. Rises. All breathe.

November Pounds My Head

The old neon above my lunch table
Buzzes like the swayback powerlines
That crisscross over the dentist's
Parking lot on late December
Nights when I take the dog out
For his final business. I look up,
Hear them crackling against cold
Air and it reminds me of another
Sound I heard, one other late night,
In a deserted downtown mall—
The Christmas lights strung through
The potted trees hissing against dense
Fog, then someone's bootsteps (following
Me?) far back in the darkness. A
Pickpocket? An angel? pausing when
I'd pause, perhaps listening, too. Don't
Ask me why, now, it gives me sadness
(What we do to each other on this earth),
It just does. But there's enough of that
To go around.   I'm thirty-five
And it's raining. Darkness comes early
Now that November pounds my head.
Yet, there's comfort, this buzzing.
At least something is happening—
The chill air that rattles in my chest.
A stranger who watches from the shadows.
The dog that follows my every step
Takes his rewards with happiness
And sleeps noisily at my hip.

The Sunday House

This swagger is not young
Robert Mitchum but last night's
Greed for more gin and lime,
More than needed to allow music
To enter through my skin.
Now I hoard the dull sunrise
With aspirins and sweet coffee
Until morning mists fade
Into December's blue, if such
December days were marketable.
Why do you do that? my ex
Once asked. I didn't know
At the time. I couldn't tell her.
Now it's the Sunday house
And the fire I managed roars
In the stove, clicking the cold
Black casement into life.
It should be easy to ignore
Compulsion and praise dawn
With an excess of clear thought.
Ah, Father, I'm sorry for your habits
That I carry on. I'm sorry
For your death these six long years,
Your gravesite tramped by Late Saints
Who steal your wreaths. I should
Have expected change to change me.
Your wife and daughter live in my
Town now. Stories run long on humor.
Once we thought you almost here.
I hold very still— how loud
The branches are this morning,
The flare of matchlight enough
To illuminate my small monastery,
The hand twitch that moves
The body forward, always forward,
The distance shortening, this swagger
To the kitchen, a practical art.

Near Water

I rose before you stirred
And stepped into the kitchen,
Not to nip once more
On the cool, plasticized Cuervo
(My head wouldn't allow it),
But to pour the coffee water
And taste a full flavor,
Stencil the pages of our crosswords,
Retrace the album of our years
Constructed from snippets
Of magazines, photos and tabloids.
The radio antenna still leaned
Against the window, balanced
For Dorsey's band snatched
From between the old growth,
Miraculously, out of Victoria.
Your crow's nest, a fishing lure,
A rusted coin, a ten of spades
And sprigs of cat's paw and moss
Seemed attentive to the river's pulse
As it pushed its gray mass
Past sleeping Mapleton.
And with coffee I stepped out
Onto the decking into morning's mist
Slung about the old cabin
And child's antique toy wagon
Of brittle paint and bell wheels—
Love, I thought of your white silk,
The stove-heated water
For our candlelit bath,
Drunk, happy in our essence
Of lemony lavender oils.
Two cabin cruisers passed by
As I stood watching the river.
Their occupants, too, holding cups,
Bundled in down and stocking caps,
Waved hello and continued their paths
Out toward open waters.
It was then I remembered where
I had once been, years ago—

Montreaux, a hostel overlooking
Lake Geneva. The skies had cleared
For the first time in three days,
The sun glittered across the lake
And sails tilled the smooth surface.
I stood in the window watching
The boats, telling myself to remember
It all, how beautiful the lake,
The sky, sails moving gracefully about,
The whiteness of the bedspread,
The walls, washbasin and tiled floors,
The crucifix and saint hung together
Above the door—Remember it all.
And I did, like now, above this
River, how memory happens best
Near water, in mist, in morning.
And what remains is a temptation
For a grand myth, not what was real—
I had a second cup of coffee,
One more smoke,
And finished one more crossword
Before you awoke.

New Year's Day

(with respects to W.C.W.)

There will be no burning of greens this year,
No roar of fire, no landscape of flame.
The sentry, once noble guardian of the parlor
Archway, now demoted to the covered porch,
Will be boxed in compost where hornets
Swirl in August heat, where the fluffed
Hunter stalks his mouse and snake.

The strings of lights have been coiled.
The gold balls wrapped, nested, secure . . .
A new home for the prolific red spider!
A safe haven for the fallen starling!
Laid where the woman with streaks
Of clay tattooed in her palms muscled
The overgrowth of blackberry bramble,
The pruned hedge, the dead yellow rose,
To make way for starts of mint and herb.

There will be no sweet smoke to give
Pause to my neighbors, to lift their snouts
Like possums testing a dangerous curb,
Tasting the acrid air, but a gift for
What was taken, perched, lit and wasted.

No. Not this year. Strong root return!
Small brother to the clearcut return!
Your epitaph is hoarfrost, moss and mold.
No fire for you, little soldier, as you lie
In your wintering manger of decay.

—for Lucena

Low Nineties

Last night your oxygen tank clicked
And steamed in the humid darkness.
This morning I'm up early, outside on
Your patio, with your navy scrapbook,
Drinking coffee and smoking low-
Tar cigarettes as your neighbor,
In Bermudas and huaraches, clips
Passages for new light in his lush
Garden. His pale peaches puff up
Like bullies. Concords seize the wicker
Trellis and scatter like shrapnel.
Sweet peas and pole beans. Straw-
Berries and nectarines. Knobby pears
Thump in the heat-whitened grass. . . .
That sailor posing in the coconut palm
Is just eighteen. On the next page
He's lost in the white, dress white
Sea on deck of the USS Parche.
Again this morning a bright red
Stain covers your nightshirt.
Your bishop brother caps your temples
In his feminine fingers and throws
Out a blessing. Unkempt, tender,
The Relief Society files in carrying
Salad bowls and casseroles. They
Twitter together on the fringe
Waiting patiently for their husbands.
Father, the waiting takes its toll.
At your viewing you'll rise and walk
Among family and friends. Your
Kind of affair. A body falls deeply
Into plaid, falls upward into blue.
Your neighbor hums, pinches leaves
Between his fingers, snaps the small weeds.
Remember Bikini Atoll? the dark visors
And flash? The needle leaped off
The dial. The husk of your submarine
Ticked like a bone clock into the next
Decade.   Today's highs, low nineties.
Small penance for the price of tithing.

You sleep upright to keep from drowning.
The sailor is always smiling. Three
Rickety M-1s will shatter the sun. Your
Neighbor huffs among his delicate genius,
Blood pump jamming in morning sweat.

Seven years ago and you still linger.
Mornings haven't been much fun since.

(1985–1992)